A balloon view of London, 1859

63 x 109 cm; shelfmark: C17: 70 London (327)

Hot air balloon ascents were a popular form of entertainment from the 1820s, and map views purporting to be drawn from balloons had a corresponding surge in popularity, although it is not known how many really were drawn from up in the sky. As the viewer is looking south, from a viewpoint above Hampstead, the map appears 'upside down' compared to most maps of London with north at the top. It was first published by J.H. Banks, who had produced an earlier view of London from the south. It ran to many editions, of which this 1859 version with hand colouring was one of at least two published by the major London mapmaker Edward Stanford; he added the hot air balloon.

Bodleian Library

Founded in 1602, the Bodleian Library is one of the oldest libraries in Britain and the largest university library in Europe. Since 1610, it has been entitled to receive a copy of every book published in the British Isles. Today, its collections exceed 13 million items and include many of the world's great library treasures.

Published by the Bodleian Library,
Broad Street, Oxford OX1 3BG
www.bodleianshop.co.uk

ISBN 978 1 85124 522 2